Friends In
A Broken World

I found myself resonating immediately with Soo-Inn's booklet—I wish it were longer! He has chosen to bare his soul in a Christian environment where testimonies are supposed to be success stories. His emphasis on community and friendship comes as a breath of fresh air in the midst of unparalleled Christian individualism— typified by the host of 'I'-choruses composed in recent times. That God should minister to us through others should convict us of our smug spiritual selfishness. Above all, the beauty of the lurking God shines brightly on every page of this monograph.

L.T. Jeyachandran, Executive Director, Ravi Zacharias International Ministries (Asia-Pacific), Singapore

Most people will not have the time or inclination to read Aelred of Rievaulx or the the other works that Soo-Inn Tan cites, but they will recognize in this book that here is a man who knows their human situation, who has walked the road of friendship himself, and who has made the rich resources of the Scriptures and the literature on friendship accessible to them. Read this and you will surely be one of those people.

Peter H. Davids, Professor of Biblical Theology, St Stephen's University, New Brunswick

There is an inviting dance between Soo-Inn's personal narrative and the narrative of Scripture in this booklet. As we eavesdrop on the conversation between the author, who serves as our friend and guide, and the Author of life, who is our ultimate Friend and true Guide, we are invited to join their dance steps of true friendship—spiritual friendship. As a pastor, husband, father, Christ-follower and fellow flawed human in these crazy times and this broken world, I cannot afford to go solo in the way I choose to live and serve. As one who has experienced the rewards of spiritual friendship in spontaneous settings as well as the spiritual friendship groups highlighted in this booklet, there has been no turning back in affirming the core message Soo-Inn is helping us discover or rediscover here. May this booklet nudge us to take those first steps…and for others to keep on dancing!

Sivin Kit, Senior Pastor, Bangsar Lutheran Church, Kuala Lumpur

When I read this book on friendship I was reminded of an ancient saying by Brigid of Kildare: "A person without a soul friend (or soul buddy) is like a body without a head". Dr Soo-Inn Tan helps us appreciate the Emmaus story in a fresh way and invites us to enter into the friendship with Jesus and with one another through his heartwarming meditation on that story. I am sure, as you read this book, your appetite for friendship and especially for friendship meals will grow irresistibly.

Koichi Ohtawa, Director, CLSK, Japan

In a day when society is more and more fragmented and loneliness is the major problem of the twenty-first century, Soo-Inn Tan's book, *Friends in a Broken World*, brings hope and encouragement. He and his wife Bernice seek to work towards seeing all Christians in one or more "friendship triads". These promote quality spiritual friendships where intimacy with one another and Christ can be found, and are a terrific way to direct our society towards health and wholeness and maturity.

Judith L. Davids, Pastoral Counsellor, St Stephen's University, New Brunswick

Friends In A Broken World

Thoughts On Friendship From the Emmaus Road

Soo-Inn Tan

GRACEWRKS

promoting spiritual friendship
in church and society

Published 2008 by Graceworks Private Limited
Ghim Moh Estate Post Office
PO Box 161, Singapore 912736
E-mail: enquiries@graceworks.com.sg
Website: www.graceworks.com.sg

Scripture quotations marked NLT are taken from the *Holy Bible, New Living Translation*, copyright © 1996, 2004. Used by permission of Tyndale House Publishers, Inc., Wheaton, IL 60189 USA. All rights reserved.

Page 51: "Thank You for Being a Friend", by Andrew Gold, recorded in his third album, *All This and Heaven Too.*

Page 52: Nouwen, Henri J. M., *Making All Things New: An Invitation to the Spiritual Life,* (New York, NY: HarperSanFrancisco, 1981), p. 82.

Cover design by Onion Design Pte Ltd

ISBN: 978-981-08-0627-9

Printed in Singapore

1 2 3 4 5 6 7 8 9 10 • 17 16 15 14 13 12 11 10 09 08

For Roson Ho
(1939 – 2008)

cousin, brother, friend

Contents

Acknowledgements

I want to thank my many friends who have helped make this book possible. The usual suspects know who they are. In particular, I want to thank Bernice, my primary friend. I have always believed marriage is meant to be missional. It is not just for the benefit of the couple. After all Adam and Eve were brought together so that they could care for God's creation. We have always believed that God brought us together so that we could be a partnership to bless others. This book is but one evidence of our calling.

Foreword

This little book packs a big punch. Simply put, spiritual friendship has the potential of changing the world, the church and especially the individual person. Genesis 2:18 tells us that we were made for this face-to-face encounter with another human being, with Christ as the hidden but influential "third". But, as Soo-Inn Tan walks through an ancient encounter of friends in the Gospel of Luke, he makes shrewd observations on how we can be diverted from true friendship by "virtual" relationships, by the modern reduction of friendship to a for-profit functional relationship and the post-modern passion for intimacy without absolute truth. This winsome book is truth strained through the personal experience of the author. In doing so it points winsomely to the friend of friends—Jesus.

R. Paul Stevens,
Professor Emeritus,
Marketplace Theology,
Regent College, Vancouver, B.C.

Introduction

❧

I have always believed in the importance of friendship. I was an only child for many years. My sister came when I was nine. We were the only two children in the family. Therefore I was "alone" for many years during the formative stages of my childhood. I remember that period of my life as a time when I often felt lonely. I am grateful for my parents, who spent as much time with me as they could. And I am especially grateful for my friends. Looking back I realize I wasn't a particularly good friend to them. Perhaps being an only child made me rather inward looking and selfish. Still, I remember the times I spent with my friends with great joy. Those moments shine in my memory as I think of my childhood.

The importance of friends was something I continued to appreciate as I moved away from childhood, to adolescence and then into adult life. I am grateful for the many good friends the Lord has sent my way. They were channels of His grace, truly undeserved because more often than not, they were better friends to me than I was to them.

My time in Regent College, Vancouver, further reinforced my conviction about the importance of relationships.[1] Regent in the '80s both emphasized and practiced community. My four years in Regent also gave me a biblical and theological framework for my understanding of the critical place of relationships for life. In particular, Regent helped me make the link between community, spiritual formation, and the authority of Scripture. Regent gave me a vision for life and ministry that has remained to this day. It taught me that God's number one priority for us is that we grow in Christ-like maturity. It also showed me that people are changed through love and truth, through relationships and Scripture.

What really cemented the vital place of friendship for me was my time in the wilderness. It was a time that began with the death of my first wife from cancer in 1993. One tragedy led to another. A second marriage ended in divorce. I lost most of my public ministry. I went into clinical depression. I had to undergo church discipline. And most of that time I had to function as a single parent, trying my best to raise my two boys. Looking back on that period of my life, I often wonder how I survived. In truth, I know the answer—I survived because of the grace of God and the encouragement of my friends.[2]

> **❝ ...people are changed through love and truth, through relationships and Scripture. ❞**

It is in your darkest moments that you discover who your true friends really are, and that God's friendship is faithful and sure.

I thought I had lost my public Christian ministry. After all, divorce was the kiss of death for any sort of public ministry in my part of the world. Again, it was the intervention of a few friends who convinced me that my ministry was not over. Since that dark period, I have started two ministries. Not surprisingly, both have emphasized the importance of friendship.

The first ministry I started was Grace@Work. Based in Malaysia, it was committed to seeing lives transformed through friendship and Scripture, a ministry carried out through speaking, writing, and mentoring. More recently, my wife Bernice and I have started Graceworks. Based in Singapore, Graceworks is committed to promoting spiritual friendship in church and society through training and publishing.

Although the two ministries are slightly different, both are committed to seeing lives transformed through community, and both see the Bible as the final authority for belief and practice. This booklet contains five meditations from a key passage that undergirds what we are trying to do. The passage is Luke 24:13-49. The first part of the passage records the encounter between the risen Christ and two of His disciples on the Emmaus Road. The rest of the passage records the appearance of Jesus to a larger group of disciples. The following meditations will focus more on the encounter on the Emmaus Road.

Here is the passage taken from the New Living Translation, second edition.[3]

The Walk to Emmaus

[13]*That same day two of Jesus' followers were walking to the village of Emmaus, seven miles from Jerusalem.* [14]*As they walked along they were talking about everything that had happened.* [15]*As they talked and discussed these things, Jesus himself suddenly came and began walking with them.* [16]*But God kept them from recognizing him.*

[17]*He asked them, "What are you discussing so intently as you walk along?"*

They stopped short, sadness written across their faces. [18]*Then one of them, Cleopas, replied, "You must be the only person in Jerusalem who hasn't heard about all the things that have happened there the last few days."*

[19]*"What things?" Jesus asked.*

"The things that happened to Jesus, the man from Nazareth," they said. *"He was a prophet who did powerful miracles, and he was a mighty teacher in the eyes of God and all the people.* [20]*But our leading priests and other religious leaders handed him over to be condemned to death, and they crucified him.* [21]*We had hoped he was the Messiah who had come to rescue Israel. This all happened three days ago.* [22]*"Then some women from our group of his followers were at his tomb early this morning, and they came back with an*

amazing report. ²³They said his body was missing, and they had seen angels who told them Jesus is alive! ²⁴Some of our men ran out to see, and sure enough, his body was gone, just as the women had said."

²⁵Then Jesus said to them, "You foolish people! You find it so hard to believe all that the prophets wrote in the Scriptures. ²⁶Wasn't it clearly predicted that the Messiah would have to suffer all these things before entering his glory?" ²⁷Then Jesus took them through the writings of Moses and all the prophets, explaining from all the Scriptures the things concerning himself.

²⁸By this time they were nearing Emmaus and the end of their journey. Jesus acted as if he were going on, ²⁹but they begged him, "Stay the night with us, since it is getting late." So he went home with them. ³⁰As they sat down to eat, he took the bread and blessed it. Then he broke it and gave it to them. ³¹Suddenly, their eyes were opened, and they recognized him. And at that moment he disappeared!

³²They said to each other, "Didn't our hearts burn within us as he talked with us on the road and explained the Scriptures to us?" ³³And within the hour they were on their way back to Jerusalem. There they found the eleven disciples and the others who had gathered with them, ³⁴who said, "The Lord has really risen! He appeared to Peter."

Jesus Appears to the Disciples

³⁵Then the two from Emmaus told their story of how Jesus had appeared to them as they were walking along the road, and how they had recognized him as he was breaking the bread. ³⁶And just as they were telling about it, Jesus himself was suddenly

standing there among them. "Peace be with you," he said. [37]But the whole group was startled and frightened, thinking they were seeing a ghost! [38]"Why are you frightened?" he asked. "Why are your hearts filled with doubt? [39]Look at my hands. Look at my feet. You can see that it's really me. Touch me and make sure that I am not a ghost, because ghosts don't have bodies, as you see that I do." [40]As he spoke, he showed them his hands and his feet.

[41]Still they stood there in disbelief, filled with joy and wonder. Then he asked them, "Do you have anything here to eat?" [42]They gave him a piece of broiled fish, [43]and he ate it as they watched.

[44]Then he said, "When I was with you before, I told you that everything written about me in the law of Moses and the prophets and in the Psalms must be fulfilled." [45]Then he opened their minds to understand the Scriptures. [46]And he said, "Yes, it was written long ago that the Messiah would suffer and die and rise from the dead on the third day. [47]It was also written that this message would be proclaimed in the authority of his name to all the nations, beginning in Jerusalem: 'There is forgiveness of sins for all who repent.' [48]You are witnesses of all these things.

[49]"And now I will send the Holy Spirit, just as my Father promised. But stay here in the city until the Holy Spirit comes and fills you with power from heaven."

(Luke 24:13-49)

Chapter 1

Lonely in a Broken World

⟨⟩

[17]He asked them, "What are you discussing so intently as you walk along?"

They stopped short, sadness written across their faces. [18]Then one of them, Cleopas, replied, "You must be the only person in Jerusalem who hasn't heard about all the things that have happened there the last few days."

[19]"What things?" Jesus asked.

"The things that happened to Jesus, the man from Nazareth," they said. "He was a prophet who did powerful miracles, and he was a mighty teacher in the eyes of God and all the people. [20]But our leading priests and other religious leaders handed him over to be condemned to death, and they crucified him. [21]We had hoped he was the Messiah who had come to rescue Israel. This all happened three days ago."

(Luke 24:17-21)

Sooner or later, in one way or another, life disappoints us. Intuitively we all seek love and meaning, and a security that ensures that we continue to enjoy both. We find both in varying degrees but discover in the end that the joys of life are ephemeral.

This truth came home to me when I lost my first wife, Hee Ling, to cancer. It happened at a time when I was on top of life. I was pastoring a major church, our second child had just arrived, and the future looked very bright. And then we discovered that Hee Ling had stage four lung cancer. She was gone within a year.

When you go through a major tragedy, your eyes are changed. Suddenly, you see that all around you are people who are also hurting and broken. You realize that a world that is so full of promise is also a world full of people with crushed hopes.

This is the lot of the two disciples we encounter on the Emmaus road in Luke 24. They had hoped that Jesus was the promised Messiah. They had come to believe that Jesus was the one that would lead Israel to a time and place where God's people would once again experience the fullness of life promised in the Scriptures. Living as they did in a day and age when many claimed to be "messiahs", they had overcome their cynicism and given their hearts to Jesus.

> **When you go through a major tragedy, your eyes are changed.**

Faith could not have come easy for the two. But they had seen Jesus' miracles. They had noted His compassion for the broken and downtrodden. They had heard His teaching. And they had come to stake their lives on this man. Now their hopes were crushed. And in what must be some of the saddest words in the Bible, we are told that they "had hoped" (v. 21). But they hoped no longer. Their hope was dead.

In their despair, the two disciples are "everyman". As Henry David Thoreau observed, "The mass of men live lives of quiet desperation" (1854). The wages of sin indeed is death and we all experience that "death" in different ways. It's just that in our time we have so many more things to distract us from our "desperation". Today, we live lives of noisy desperation. What is worse, we also live in times of greater loneliness and alienation.

In his book *Vital Friends*, Tom Rath notes that:

> …friendships are among the most fundamental of human needs. The fact is, we are biologically predisposed to this need for relationships, and our environment accentuates this every day. Without friends, it is very difficult for us to get by, let alone thrive.[1]

We will examine friendship in more detail later but we note that at least the two disillusioned disciples on the Emmaus road had each other. The rest of us may not be as fortunate.

More and more we live lives disconnected from others, lives bereft of the succour of friendship. Technologies meant to connect us result in fewer face-to-face connections and the loss of intimacy in our day-to-day relationships. John L. Locke observes this trend in his book, *The De-Voicing of Society*:

> Computer-assisted communication is coming on like a steamroller, flattening intimate forms of self-expression. Justifying the cost and time associated with business trips will get harder, especially when the available communication systems were bought in order to obviate such travel. Eventually, meeting or knowing someone with whom we work will be viewed as a coincidence.
>
> A clock is ticking on our personal lives, and our communities, and our civic institutions. How much longer can we and our communities prosper with so little personal warmth and trust?[2]

Locke wrote in 1998. I wonder if he could have foreseen how ubiquitous the Internet would become and how acute would be the experience of loneliness in modern society.

More than ever we need to recover a healthy understanding of friendship and its practice. More than ever we need our friends. This is particularly true for those who are followers of Jesus Christ for we follow a Lord who says, "…you are my friends" (John 15:15b). Indeed, the first friend we need in a broken world is Jesus. [♥]

Chapter 2

Jesus, Our Divine Friend

⁓

¹³That same day two of Jesus' followers were walking to the village of Emmaus, seven miles from Jerusalem. ¹⁴As they walked along they were talking about everything that had happened. ¹⁵As they talked and discussed these things, Jesus himself suddenly came and began walking with them. ¹⁶But God kept them from recognizing him.

(Luke 24:13-16)

When my father died, my friend took leave and came for the funeral. He lives in Kuala Lumpur and dad was to be buried in Penang, about 250 miles away. My friend was one of the directors of a major merchant bank and his time was at a premium. But he was also my friend and so he made the time to be with me as I said my goodbyes to my dad. It's just the thing that friends do.

Friends commit themselves to care for each other. If Jesus is our friend, as He claims to be (John 15:15b), we would not expect Him to do any less. And so we should not be surprised that He takes the initiative to go to the two disillusioned disciples on the Emmaus road and begins to walk alongside them.

The two disciples were not looking for Him. They thought He was dead and buried. There was nothing in the disciples' actions that qualified them for the divine friendship that they were to receive. Jesus saw the disciples in pain. He went to them. Friendship cannot be earned or bought. It is a gift freely given. And Jesus gives Himself freely to the two disciples. He was their friend.

> **"Friendship cannot be earned or bought. It is a gift freely given."**

Jesus had made the ultimate gift of friendship a few days before this fateful encounter on the Emmaus road. He had already said "there is no greater love than to lay down one's life for one's friends" (John 15:13). And He had done exactly that. He had given Himself, going to the Cross for a humankind dead in sin. He was a true friend.

God has been doing this throughout history. In Exodus 3:1-10, God shows His "friend heart" when He reveals that He is aware of the pain of His people, and that He will take the initiative to "come down to rescue them." There is nothing here about the Israelites "going up" to God's level to earn their redemption. What true friend would expect that? When you hear that a friend is in trouble you go to him or her to help. God "came down" to deliver Israel from Egypt. He "came down" to the Cross to rescue us from sin and death. The promise of divine friendship shines as the only true hope for those of us who live in this broken world.

R. Paul Stevens has this to say about friendship with God:

> Friendship between God and humankind is the ultimate goal of God's grace and the spiritual journey, as modeled by Moses with whom God spoke on Sinai "face to face" as a man speaks with his friend (Exodus 33:11). Abraham was a friend of God (Isaiah 41:8; James 2:23), and Job hungered for God's friendship more than he desired relief from his suffering: "Oh for the days when I was in my prime, when God's intimate friendship blessed my house" (Job 29:4). Satan's question addressed the heart of Job's friendship with God: "Does Job fear God for nothing?" (Job 1:9). Friendship, even friendship with God is not for anything. It has no utilitarian value. That is, our relationship to God should not be a commercial relationship in which we exchange piety for spiritual, even eternal, benefits.[1]

Divine friendship helps us to understand friendship

as it should be. As Stevens points out, true friendship is non-utilitarian. We don't befriend someone *so that* we can get something out of that person. Friends are enjoyed for their own sakes. Friendship is also personal; it is a face-to-face, intimate relationship. If needed, we will sacrificially help our friends. It is not something that our friends expect of us. It is something we expect of ourselves. It's what friends do. And on the Emmaus road, it is what Jesus did for the two disciples.

However, we note that at first, the two disciples could not recognize that it was Jesus who had come to them. In fact we are told that "God kept them from recognizing him" (v. 16).[2] If Jesus had revealed His identity too early, the two disciples would have found relief for their emotional anguish—and would have learnt nothing. Instead, their pain put them in a teachable stance and Jesus was able to give them a walking seminar, helping the disciples to be rooted in the Word, something that had to happen if they were to be able to live and serve after Jesus' ascension.

True love must be tough love. If we truly love our friends, we will give them what they need, which may not be what they want. Jesus may have practiced tough love but He is utterly clear as to what He is trying to do in the lives of the disciples. Because of His ministry, the two disciples move from tears (v. 17), to joy (v. 52) and to mission (vv. 47-49). Jesus' friendship brings healing and purpose. And that is what He wants to do in our lives if we will allow Him to. ♥

Chapter 3

Divine Friendship and Human Friendship

❧

[13]That same day two of Jesus' followers were walking to the village of Emmaus, seven miles from Jerusalem. [14]As they walked along they were talking about everything that had happened.

(Luke 24:13-14)

In the early days of my widowerhood, I was lost. Nothing in my life prior to that point had prepared me for the loss of a spouse. My doctrinal framework remained unchanged, and my faith, though shaken, was intact. But doctrine is cold comfort for a new widower. A good friend, Lee Hong Kwang,[1] would come by once a week and take me out for dim-sum and tea. He didn't say much but he was there. He practiced the ministry of "presence" and, in his presence, I experienced the presence of Christ.

The best human friendships should mediate the friendship of God. As we see in the experience of the two disciples on the Emmaus road, when true friends walk together, Jesus comes alongside. Therefore if we take divine friendship seriously, we must also take human friendship seriously. This type of friendship that interweaves the divine and the human is what writers like James M. Houston call "spiritual friendship", "…a friendship in the company of Christ".[2]

Commenting on the work of Aelred of Rievaulx, Paul J. Wadell has this to say about spiritual friendship:

> Every friendship is formed around shared goods that identify the friendship and help the friends understand the life and purpose of the friendship. In spiritual friendship the principal good is a mutual love for Christ and a desire to grow together in Christ. This is what distinguishes spiritual friendship from other relationships. In spiritual friendships the friends are centred in Christ, they seek Christ, and they strive to live according to Christ. Through their friendship they want to help one another live a godly and holy life. They want each other to be resplendent in goodness.[3]

At a fundamental level, we all need friends to be truly human. In his book *Social Intelligence*, Daniel Goleman reports:

> Among people around the world,

nourishing relationships are the single most universally agreed-upon feature of the good life. While the specifics vary from culture to culture, all people everywhere deem warm connections with others to be the core feature of "optimal human existence."[4]

Much earlier, and with much more economy of words, the writer of Ecclesiastes had already observed the logic of friendship:

> *Two people are better off than one, for they can help each other succeed. If one person falls, the other can reach out and help. But someone who falls alone is in real trouble. Likewise, two people lying close together can keep each other warm. But how can one be warm alone? A person standing alone can be attacked and defeated, but two can stand back-to-back and conquer. Three are even better, for a triple-braided cord is not easily broken.*
> (Ecclesiastes 5:9-12)

The two disciples on the Emmaus road may have gotten their theology wrong, but they had gotten one thing right—they understood the importance of friendship. In their moments of faith and doubt they had each other. And the quality of their friendship is seen in the fact that they were allowed to share their strongest emotions in each other's presence (v. 17). They were also partners in blessing others (vv. 28-31).

Human friendship cannot replace divine friendship. The two disciples had each other and were able to share their common grief. But they had no real solutions to their despair till Jesus came to them. So while we work to strengthen the friendships in our lives, and in the lives of others, we need to continue to nurture our friendship with Christ and introduce others to His friendship. Jesus continues to be the one that says:

> *Look! I stand at the door and knock. If you hear my voice and open the door, I will come in, and we will share a meal together as friends.*
> (Revelation 3:20)

The two disciples on the Emmaus road invited Jesus in and became His friends.

If human friendship cannot replace divine friendship, neither can divine friendship replace human friendship. Even though Adam had an unsullied friendship with God in the Garden of Eden before the Fall, it was still not good for him to be without human companionship (Genesis 2:18). Marriage is one way that this need for companionship is met. And I thank God for my wife Bernice who, with her generous love, nurtures my soul and helps me be all that I should be.

The Bible also makes mention of true friends, the type that "sticks closer than a brother" (Proverbs

18:24). I am grateful that the Lord has brought such friends into my life as well. These friends have not excused my sins and my failures. But they have stood by me, even during the tumultuous moments in my journey, and they have done this even though it has cost them time, money and reputation. They have shared my burdens (Galatians 6:2). They have encouraged me (1Thessalonians 5:11). And they have motivated me to "acts of love and good works" (Hebrews 10:24). They have been there for me, and because they were there for me they reminded me that Christ was there too. ⟨♥⟩

> **"So while we work to strengthen the friendships in our lives, and in the lives of others, we need to continue to nurture our friendship with Christ..."**

Chapter 4

Friendship and Truth

❧

^{25}Then Jesus said to them, "You foolish people! You find it so hard to believe all that the prophets wrote in the Scriptures. ^{26}Wasn't it clearly predicted that the Messiah would have to suffer all these things before entering his glory?" ^{27}Then Jesus took them through the writings of Moses and all the prophets, explaining from all the Scriptures the things concerning himself.

(Luke 24:25-27)

I was sharing with a friend that I was struggling with a decision to leave the pastorate to take on a position in a Christian parachurch organization where I would be focusing on teaching and writing. He said, "You are just so-so as a pastor. You should focus on teaching. You would make a better teacher." I felt both disappointed and relieved; disappointed because I was confronted by my limitations as a pastor, and relieved that I might be free to pursue a position that would be more in line with my gifts and temperament.

The above exchange took place a long time ago. My thoughts on what it means to be a pastor and a teacher have long since evolved. And I am much clearer now as to what my vocation is. But I will never forget my friend's honest feedback. True friends tell you the truth.

Which may explain Jesus' strong words to the two disciples. Here were two people in deep grief. Surely they deserved comfort and encouragement. Instead Jesus rebukes them (v. 25). Why? Because that was what they needed—the truth.

Again, I am certain that Jesus had in mind a time when He would no longer be there to tutor the disciples personally. There would come a time when He would be "taken up to heaven" (Luke 24:51). The two disciples, and all disciples hence, had to learn to build their lives on the Word illumined by His Spirit. The two disciples needed comfort, but that comfort would have to come from their faith in a proper understanding of the Scriptures. Therefore Jesus needed to confront them with the truth, unpleasant though that may have been. It's what friends do.

Paul J. Wadell captures this aspect of friendship well when he writes:

> Spiritual friends do not see us changing in ways that are harmful and keep silent.

They are willing to be truthful with us because they care for us and do not want us to imperil the most promising possibility of our lives: our friendship with God. Such friends are rare because it takes courage to speak the truth when doing so risks our being misunderstood or rejected by another. It is much easier to flatter our friends than be truthful with them, and one of the dangers in any friendship is that we begin consoling one another with comforting deceptions instead of challenging one another with the truth.[1]

True friends tell us what we need to know and not what we want to hear. This will include gently pointing out our failures and lapses, and the dismantling of our self-deceptions. These are the wounds of a friend and Scripture tells us that "Wounds from a sincere friend are better than many kisses from an enemy" (Proverbs 27:6). Indeed, Paul reminds us that we must "speak the truth in love" if we are to mature in Christ (Ephesians 4:15). I shall always be grateful to the friends who told me the truth even when it was tough to speak and tough to listen.

> **True friends tell us what we need to know and not what we want to hear.**

Speaking the truth in love also includes helping people see their strengths and gifts. When friends speak the truth in love "they may encourage us to develop talents we did not know we had or to take chances we would otherwise avoid".[2] We want to be honest with our friends, and we want honesty from our friends because friends are committed to helping each other be all that they were meant to be.

The true soul friend will not accept our self-deception but will gently and firmly confront us with our soul blindness. Soul friends want each other to settle for nothing short of becoming the whole and holy person they were meant to be.[3]

The first act of friendship is grace and acceptance. Jesus did not wait for the two disciples to "get it" before He reached out to them in love. Friendship must be a safe place where people know they are loved unconditionally. Only then can friends lower their masks and be who they really are.

But true love desires the best of the one being loved. Therefore, secure in a relationship of grace, friends help each other align their lives to God's truth. But this must always be done gently.

> *Dear brothers and sisters, if another believer is overcome by some sin, you who are godly should gently and humbly help that person back onto the right path. And be careful not to fall into the same temptation yourself. Share each other's burdens, and in this way obey the law of Christ.*
>
> (Galatians 5:1-2)

If the modern world made friendships functional, the post-modern world hungers for an intimacy that is not rooted in truth. Neither will do. True friendships can only be built on the foundations of grace and truth. 🖤

Chapter 5
The Practice of Friendship

⁂

²⁸By this time they were nearing Emmaus and the end of their journey. Jesus acted as if he were going on, ²⁹but they begged him, "Stay the night with us, since it is getting late." So he went home with them. ³⁰As they sat down to eat, he took the bread and blessed it. Then he broke it and gave it to them. ³¹Suddenly, their eyes were opened, and they recognized him. And at that moment he disappeared!

(Luke 24:28-31)

The three of us used to meet up for lunch once a month. It was a commitment. We made sure it happened. I was the only one in full-time church-related work. My other two friends worked in the marketplace. But we all knew the critical importance of spiritual friendship. And we all knew that we had to meet up face to face on a regular basis for the friendship to work. As we shared food, we shared our lives. We would give each other updates on what was happening in our work, our families, our churches, and in our own personal pilgrimages. We would seek each other's thoughts when we faced key decisions. Sometimes we would share about temptations we were facing. Sometimes we confessed our sins. We were all online and we kept in touch by email regularly. But we knew that nothing replaced our face-to-face meetings over a meal.

The climax of the encounter between Jesus and the two disciples on the Emmaus road was a meal. The two disciples invited Jesus to their home. And they shared a meal. Interestingly, though Jesus was the guest, He acted as though He was the host. Perhaps the two disciples recognized that Jesus was some kind of spiritual teacher and allowed Him to "say grace". What is interesting is that it was only when they had settled down to a meal that they finally recognized their mysterious companion was Jesus. Perhaps it is only when we have slowed down to the pace of a "sit-down"[1] meal that we can begin to really connect.

> **"Clearly, the Bible puts a high premium on face-to-face relationships."**

The Bible has always recognized the importance of both face-to-face relationships and eating together. In 2 John 12, we read:

> *I have much more to say to you, but I don't want to do it with paper and ink. For I hope to visit you soon and talk with you face to face. Then our joy will be complete.*

There is a level of communication that is only possible face to face, a level of communication that makes possible a special level of joy. In 1 Thessalonians 3:10, Paul prays that the Lord will allow him to see the Thessalonian Christians face to face as there were certain spiritual blessings that could only be conveyed personally. Clearly, the Bible puts a high premium on face-to-face relationships. We need to bear this in mind as we seek to build genuine friendships in a world where communication technology often makes communication less personal.

Since the Bible sees personal communication as critical for human interaction, we are not surprised that the Bible also understands eating together as very important. Indeed, the primary act for the church gathered in New Testament times was eating together. Writing about the practices of the early house churches, Wolfgang Simson reminds us:

> The house church—is a table community, sharing real food. The Lord's Supper was a substantial supper with a symbolic meaning, not a symbolic supper with a substantial meaning. As they were simply eating a lamb together, it dawned on them what this was all about: humans having dinner with God.[2]

We have already seen the integral connection between our friendship with God and our friendship with each other. The Lord's Supper expresses and cements both these relationships. As Gordon T. Smith writes:

> In the Lord's Supper, we are not merely eating; we are eating *together.* There is a companionship with Christ, surely, but it is a communal event. We are in fellowship with Christ, and we are in fellowship with one another. Table fellowship, while declaring that we are in fellowship with Christ and one another, also cultivates and enables this fellowship. When we eat together as families and friends, we simultaneously affirm our shared identity and cultivate our unity....The Lord's Supper is an act of Holy Communion— with Christ and with one another.[3]

What Smith says about the Lord's Supper can also be said about every meal that Christians share in the Name of Christ, where they are conscious of His presence. In fact, when Christian friends sit down to share an actual meal, aware of His presence and His goodness, they may be doing something more akin to the Lord's Supper celebrations of the early church than the highly ceremonial Communion services we see in most churches today.

God made humankind with bodies. We are not disembodied souls. Therefore authentic human interaction should involve our bodies. True friendships cannot be solely virtual. They must be nurtured regularly by occasions where friends occupy the same space and time. Like when the two disciples on the Emmaus road were walking together. Like when they sat down for a meal. ♥

Conclusion

❧

Friendship is grossly underrated. At first glance it appears soft and inconsequential. Yet when the Messiah came, He called us His friends (John 15:14). Perhaps there is more to friendship than meets the eye. In her book *Turning to One Another*, Margaret J. Wheatley writes:

> Human conversation is the most ancient and easiest way to cultivate the conditions for change—personal change, community and organizational change, planetary change. If we can sit together and talk about what's important to us, we begin to come alive. We share what we see, what we feel, and we listen to what others see and feel.[1]

Wheatley goes on to cite various examples of what can happen when ordinary people come together in community. One example she offers is the rise of the Solidarity movement in Poland:

> Solidarity in Poland began with conversation—less than a dozen workers in a

Gdansk shipyard speaking to each other about their despair, their need for change, their need for freedom. In less than a month, Solidarity grew to 9.5 million workers. There was no e-mail then, just people talking to each other about their own needs, and finding their needs shared by millions of fellow citizens. At the end of the month, all 9.5 million of them acted as one voice for change. They shut down the country.[2]

Perhaps simple friendship is not as inconsequential after all.

The need for "personal change, community and organizational change, planetary change" has never been greater. Daily, we are reminded that we live in a broken world. We also see that any help that comes from politics and economics is at best limited. And the violence of wars and terrorism is no real answer. It is clear that the help humankind needs lies elsewhere and, more and more, we suspect that the real help we need is somehow rooted in relationships.

> **We acknowledge the power of human friendship. But we also see that any chance of radical and permanent change lies in our embracing the saving friendship of God.**

Our suspicions are confirmed by the lessons we learn from the Emmaus road encounter between the two disciples and the risen Christ. And the first lesson is this: no change is possible without the friendship of Christ. Here, we would go one step further than writers like Margaret J. Wheatley. We acknowledge the power of human friendship. But we also see that any chance of radical and permanent change lies in our embracing the saving friendship of God.

The Emmaus Road encounter teaches us that there is a clear link between divine friendship and human friendship. Indeed, evangelism at its best is inviting people to the table of the Lord where Jesus awaits as host to feed us with what we truly need. And discipleship at its best is simply the commitment to follow Christ in the company of friends.[3]

However, we need to bear in mind two things: true friendship of any sort must be based on truth and honesty, and friendships cannot survive, much less thrive, if we do not sustain them with regular face-to-face interaction. In the words of James M. Houston:

> I believe that, rather than professional pursuits or even writing meaningful books, the prime action of our lives is the face-to-face encounter with others, bringing God's presence into their lives by being "living apostles …".[4]

The need for life-giving friendships has never been greater. David G. Benner believes that the optimal size for spiritual friendship groups "is probably between three and five members".[5] I have a dream— that every believer will be part of at least one spiritual friendship group, and that as they journey with their friends, they will find a community where they will obtain real encouragement as they face the challenges of life, and real encouragement to be all that they should be. I have a dream that everyone will find the friendship that he or she needs, as a critical step to finding wholeness in a broken world. ❤

Endnotes

Introduction

1. I was a full-time student at Regent College, Vancouver, from 1981 to 1985.

2. This phrase and the wisdom that it summarizes comes from Gordon T. Smith's book, *Courage & Calling* (Downer's Grove, IL: InterVarsity press, 1999), p.124.

3. I chose the NLT as my basic translation for its accessibility and readability.

Chapter 1

1. Tom Rath, *Vital Friends*, (New York, NY: Gallup Press, 2006), p.15.

2. John L. Locke, *The De-Voicing of Society*, (New York, NY: Simon & Schuster, 1998), p. 194.

Chapter 2

1. R. Paul Stevens. "Friendship", *The Complete Book of Everyday Christianity*, edited by Robert Banks & R. Paul Stevens (Downers Grove, IL: InterVarsity Press, 1997), p.439.

2. The original Greek merely says "...they were kept from recognizing him". However, it is implied that it was God who kept them from recognizing Him, and so the NLT has put "God" in its translation.

Chapter 3

1. Lee Hong Kwang was a key leader in the Malaysian Brethren churches. He has since gone home to the Lord. I miss him.

2. James M. Houston, *Joyful Exiles*, (Downers Grove, IL: InterVarsity Press, 2006), p.167.

3. Paul J. Wadell, *Becoming Friends*, (Grand Rapids, MI: Brazos Press, 2002), pp. 107-108.

4. Daniel Goleman, *Social Intelligence*, (New York, NY: Bantam Press, 2007), p.312.

Chapter 4

1. Paul J. Wadell, *Becoming Friends*, (Grand Rapids, MI: Brazos Press, 2002), p.115.

2. Ibid., p.69.

3. David G. Benner, *Sacred Companions*, (Downers Grove, IL: InterVarsity Press, 2002), p.70.

Chapter 5

1. In Jesus' time, they reclined at the table for their meals.

2. Wolfgang Simson, *Houses That Change the World*,

(Carlisle, Cumbria, UK: OM Publishing, 1998), p.82.

3. Gordon T. Smith, *A Holy Meal*, (Grand Rapids, MI: Baker Academic, 2005), p.47.

Conclusion

1. Margaret J. Wheatley, *Turning to One Another*, (San Francisco, CA: Berrett-Koehler Publishers, INC., 2002), p.3.

2. Ibid., p.22.

3. I am indebted to Richard Lamb and his book, *The Pursuit of God in the Company of Friends*, (Downers Grove, IL: InterVarsity Press, 2003) for this image of the Christian life.

4. James M. Houston, *Joyful Exiles*, (Downers Grove, IL: InterVarsity Press, 2006), p.177.

5. David G. Benner, *Sacred Companions*, (Downers Grove, IL: InterVarsity Press, 2002), p.174.

Appendix A

❦

(The following essay first appeared as a weekly column that I send out via email.)

The Power of Three
by Soo-Inn Tan, 27 Sep 2004

They were about ten years my junior. But we were at ages where such age differences didn't really matter. The three of us would meet up for an extended lunch once a month. As we enjoyed the diverse cuisines available in Malaysia, we would, on purpose, ask each other three key questions:

(1) How is your family life? *(2)* How is your church life? *(3)* How is your work life?

Each one would take his turn to answer while the others listened attentively. We would affirm and caution if needed but there was a lot more listening than speaking going on.

Occasionally one of us would be facing a key decision and we would lay it before the rest for their feedback. Sometimes there would be admissions of sin and failure. The fact that we were all guys who shared similar temptations and failures, helped sustain the confessional dimension of the group.

The three of us came from different churches. We had met while I was a freshman pastor, and they were seniors at a local university. My role had moved quickly from minister to friend. And now, many years later, we were spiritual friends. Our "friendship triad" was a key source of spiritual sustenance.

In his book *The Voice of Jesus*, Gordon T. Smith writes about the power of spiritual friendship:

> "...along the way, God will grant us the privilege of genuine friendship with one, two or three individuals who are truly codiscerners. They allow us to be individual; they free us to be other. Yet they also enable us to overcome our radical aloneness. As a friend, we have the opportunity to be the presence and voice of Jesus to others, enabling them to know they are loved, because we demonstrate it and free them to experience the inner assurance of God's love."

Mark
Janet

Beth K

Most of us are too familiar with "radical aloneness". This is indeed ironic for followers of a faith that proclaims the crucial place of community and fellowship.

Most Sunday worship services focus more on our individual encounter with God, albeit in the company of others. On a good day we come away inspired by a good sermon, grateful for the opportunity to lift our hearts to God through our singing. But Sunday worship services are not geared for spiritual friendship.

Many churches recognize this lack of fellowship in the church's big meetings and run some form of cell groups. Unfortunately, few cell groups allow for in-depth relationships. Some are more task oriented than relationship oriented. The purpose of such cell groups is to support the evangelistic efforts of the church.

And the inclusive nature of most cell groups means that they are made up of people of diverse spiritual and personal maturities. One thinks twice about opening one's soul in groups like these, not sure how our sharing will be received or how the information will be used.

Still, membership in a cell group is better than merely participating in a church's big group activities. At least we will begin to know some church members a little better. But where will we go to be who we truly are?

Some of us will seek out spiritual directors. We seek out folks who will help guide us in our spiritual journey. Spiritual directors are listeners above all; people who accept us as we are and who will listen to our lives to help us hear what the Lord is saying.

But spiritual directors are not that easy to find. Indeed many of us may come from spiritual traditions that are only just beginning to understand the need for, and the work of, spiritual directors. But all of us understand the need for friends.

Hence I am hoping that all Christians should be part of one or more "friendship triads." Why groups of three? Why not quads? Or dyads? Of course there is no biblical reason why it shouldn't be dyads or quads. Many do find quality friendship in dyads and quads or groupings of other numbers.

Practically speaking, groups that are too big tend to lower the level of intimacy. And in today's highly mobile world, it is extremely difficult to find a common meeting time for groups with too many members.

In his book *Transforming Discipleship*, Greg Ogden gives a number of reasons why a triad is better than a dyad for the purposes of spiritual friendship. (He sees dyads as more appropriate for intensive spiritual mentoring.) Among the reasons he gives are:

> "There is a shift from hierarchical to relational."

"The triad naturally creates a come-alongside mutual journey. The focus is not so much on the discipler as it is upon Christ as the one toward whom all are directing their lives."

"There is a shift from dialogue to dynamic interchange."

"With one-on-one, there are only four possible combinations of communication. Each individual has a unique perspective and an opinion about the other person's perspective. When you add a third party, the number of possible interplays of communication increases to ten."

It is also interesting to note that Jesus worked with groups of seventy (Luke 10:1), twelve (Luke 6:12-16), and three (Luke 9:28).

I would suggest then, that most of us should be in one or more friendship triads. It is a simple and manageable way to experience the spiritual friendship we all need.

If you are not in one, you may want to start a triad. First pray about two people you want to invite to make up such a triad. Members of the same sex are preferable for the kind of intimacy hoped for. Introduce them to the purposes and mechanics of the friendship triad.

While there should be a minimum of rules, such friendship triads should be characterized by three biblical injunctions:

1. Accept one another (Romans 15:7).
2. Bear one another's burdens (Galatians 6:2).
3. Encourage one another to love and good works (Hebrews 10:24).

(other "Let us" in Heb?)

Covenant to meet together on a regular basis. Once a month is minimum. When you meet, connect using the three questions about family, church and work.

You can come up with your own set of questions of course. One that Gordon T. Smith uses is: "Since we met last, what have been your joys and sorrows?" He saw the question as an exercise where he and his friends learned how to "rejoice and mourn with one another" (Romans 12:15).

You need to review the life of the group periodically to see if the group should continue, or if the season of the group is over, and it should come to an end. Groups come and go but the need for spiritual friendship will always be there. When a group ends we will have to think about the possibility of starting new ones.

We need a revolution of spiritual friendship in these lonely, godless days. Here is a simple way to do it. Have you tried a triad?

"Thank you for being a friend,
Traveled down the road and back again,
Your heart is true, you're a pal and a
confidant."

(Andrew Gold)

Friendship, marriage, family, religious life, and every other form of community is solitude greeting solitude, spirit speaking to spirit, and heart calling to heart. It is the grateful recognition of God's call to share life together and the joyful offering of a hospitable space where the recreating power of God's Spirit can become manifest. Thus all forms of life together can become ways to reveal to each other the real presence of God in our midst.

Henri J. M. Nouwen